LEYLAND LORRIES

BILL REID

AMBERLEY

Acknowledgements

The majority of the pictures used in this book are from my own camera, or from years of collecting lorry and bus photos. I would like to thank Wobbe Reitsma, Ian Lawson, Pat Crang, Gyles Carpenter, Chris Baron, Gillies Watson, Alex Syme, and the late Ken Durston for their contributions, and assistance.

First published 2017

Amberley Publishing
The Hill, Stroud
Gloucestershire, GL5 4EP

www.amberley-books.com

Copyright © Bill Reid, 2017

The right of Bill Reid to be identified as the Author of this work has been asserted in accordance with the Copyrights, Designs and Patents Act 1988.

ISBN 978 1 4456 6744 7 (print)
ISBN 978 1 4456 6745 4 (ebook)

British Library Cataloguing in Publication Data. A catalogue record for this book is available from the British Library.

Typesetting by Amberley Publishing.
Printed in the UK.

Introduction

The roots of Leyland lorries began in the late nineteenth century when Lancashire Steam Motor Co. was formed in the town of Leyland by James Sumner and members of the Spurrier family. Their first steam lorry took to the road in 1897 and proved to be a success, allowing expansion and the takeover of a neighbouring steam lorry producer – Coulthards, in Preston.

Petrol-engined lorry production started in 1904 and were produced alongside the original steam-powered vehicles. With the takeover of Coulthards the company name was changed to Leyland Motors Ltd, and two new petrol-engined chassis increased the range of vehicles in production. Further expansion took place at Leyland and various models with the petrol engine came into production.

A War Office subsidy scheme in 1912 was instrumental in increasing production of petrol-engined lorries through a buyer's discount and subsidy for the following three years, which meant in the event of war the vehicles would be requisitioned for the armed forces. These favourable conditions brought about the A type 3-ton lorry, later known as the RAF type.

On the outbreak of the First World War, Leyland production of the A type as a military vehicle commenced within a fortnight and in 1915 all production of the A type was on behalf of the Royal Flying Corps, later to become the Royal Air Force.

By the end of the war there was a surplus of military vehicles, with thousands being sold by auction, which prompted Leyland Motors to consider their sales and reputation. Many of the surplus Leylands were bought by the company and rebuilt in a newly acquired factory at Kingston-upon-Thames and offered for sale, rather than having them sold in poor condition. Altruistic, perhaps, but preserving the now well-established name.

The 1920s brought an expansion in the range with various types for different load weights, alongside bus chassis that were to revolutionise the double-deck bus design. Steam lorry production had ceased by this time.

The 1930s saw a further expansion of the Leyland range and heavier lorry chassis were being produced, which saw the beginning of maximum weight lorries on 2, 3, and 4 axles. These lorries had larger engines – all produced by Leyland – of petrol or diesel design, bringing a degree of integration to the range. A range of lighter chassis was also in production.

By 1939 the Second World War had broken out and the Leyland factories were turned over to war material production, but a 3-axle chassis was built throughout the war as a general service lorry. Much of Leyland's wartime production was of the Comet tank.

On the return to peace in 1945, Leyland embarked on new designs, which saw the light of day as a new range of lorries again based on maximum-capacity 2-, 3-, and 4-axle types, which took Leyland through the 1950s. The engines were also Leyland designs and were to be found in the contemporary bus and coach ranges.

As in the 1930s, Leyland saw a need for a smaller range of lorries, but not to the same extent of production. Many of the UK car manufacturers were, by then, producing ranges of cheap lorries and competing in the lightweight market. Leyland perceived a market share in the 6- to 7-ton range and entered that sector with the Comet lorry, which was to become a long standing model.

The late 1950s saw the Leyland lorry model range progress in design into the Power-Plus range, and in 1964 – after a favourable change in legislation allowing larger and heavier lorries – the new Freightline range was introduced. A new cab design, known as the Ergomatic, was introduced at the same time, appearing in AEC and Albion lorries, which had become part of the Leyland Motors empire.

By the late 1960s, early 1970s, the European manufacturers – such as Volvo and Scania – were making sales inroads in the UK with high-power engines and superior cabs, which saw a decline in sales across the UK manufacturers. Leyland responded rather slowly to this competition and offered new engines, but carried on with the same cab; now seen to be dated and small by the European cab standards.

Also in the late 1960s, Leyland Motors merged with British Motor Holdings (BMH), which was mainly a corporate producer of cars, in a government-backed bid to sustain this large producer. This brought the BMC commercial ranges of vans and lorries into the Leyland portfolio, which then gave a sales coverage from 1.5 tonnes to weights similar to existing Leyland models. The spread of vehicle types was vast and a degree of rationalisation was inevitable.

In 1972 the existing BMC and Albion lorries were to be badged as Leyland, with Albion production being transferred to the former BMC factory, at Bathgate, Scotland.

By that time the Leyland range, which also included Guy Motors, was in need of a new design. This was introduced in the late 1970s as the T45 range; an integrated design that saw interchangeability and a family likeness between the smallest model – the RoadRunner – all the way up to the heavyweight Roadtrain artics. The T45 range did well and was a good competitor to the European imports, but Leyland's fortunes were to change radically. Cash was being drained at an alarming rate to keep the car manufacturing side viable, eventually leading up to a split of the consortium into smaller groups for sale.

DAF Trucks of Holland bought the Leyland lorry part of the consortium, and production was thereafter badged as Leyland DAF. The fortunes of DAF were to go sour soon after the purchase of the Leyland lorry assets, and PACCAR of America bought the entire DAF company. The Leyland name disappeared, never being used after the PACCAR acquisition.

The Leyland legacy is the number of lorries, buses, and coaches to be found in preservation today. It was a very popular vehicle range throughout its production time, with a high degree of interchangeability of components, such as the engines and running gear. From a nostalgic point of view there was little to surpass the sound of a Leyland engine on idle speed, or at full power.

Early production of steam vehicles by the Lancashire Steam Motor Company were designed on the horse-drawn vehicle style, with the steam engine behind the driver, driving the rear wheels by chain. The wheels were similar to cart wheels. The front wheels were a smaller diameter to allow steering action, but this appears to be limited.

The Lancashire steam wagon evolved into a more familiar steam wagon style, with the boiler at the front and the engine underneath the chassis, still using chain drive. This old advert shows a Class H wagon for 5 tons with broad steel wheels; in keeping with the loaded weight.

A photograph showing an H Class Lancashire steam wagon when presumably new and out on test somewhere near the Leyland factory. It appears to be carrying test weights, but there is no indication of the load weight.

An H Class which was been exported to Australia and has been preserved in a rather gaudy yellow and red colour scheme. The boiler, engine, and chain drive to the rear axle are clearly visible as in the advertising picture at Fig 2.

This is an early petrol-engined X Type 3-tonner. It had a 6-litre 4 cylinder Crossley engine, which, combined with the solid tyres, must have given a rough ride on the basic bench seat. The high open cab would have given scant weather protection.

A rather grainy picture taken from a Leyland slide, which would have otherwise been thrown away at the closure of the Leyland Bathgate factory. It shows a development of the original 'overtype' petrol engine lorry with the driver placed above the engine, allowing more load-carrying space. A precursor of the modern day high cab!

Leyland lorry production continued and in the early 1910s the government introduced a scheme whereby buyers of lorries could receive a subsidy. In turn the owners were obliged to maintain the lorries in good condition and, in the event of the outbreak of war, would deliver the vehicle for wartime service. This led to the Leyland produced Subsidy chassis for 3-ton loads.

The Subsidy chassis was later known as the RAF type as all wartime production was allocated to the Royal Flying Corps, soon to be renamed the Royal Air Force (RAF). These lorries were used in all manner of duties, from general transport to medical and dental vans.

On the cessation of hostilities in 1918 there was an enormous stockpile of military lorries of many makes, surplus to requirements. As these lorries were being sold by auction – some in poor condition – Leyland Motors opened a factory at Kingston-on-Thames to refurbish or rebuild Leyland chassis as a means of retaining their good reputation. This furniture van may have been one of the rebuilds.

Some of the RAF types have survived into preservation and this example shows a tipper with modernised wheels and tyres. The overall size of the lorry is well scaled by the gentleman studying it on the right of the picture.

In the early 1920s Leyland produced the A1 type for 2-ton loads. This example for a builder on Bury shows its unladen weight of 3 tons 12 cwt and capable of 6 tons on the rear axle; a substantial lorry for only 2 tons carrying capacity.

Exported to Australia, this A1 Type has survived into preservation in its original condition, with cast-steel spoked wheels and solid rubber tyres. The cab accommodation is easily seen, while the lack of headlamps may mean an unfinished project.

The RAF type was a rugged lorry and many existed as working lorries long after their manufacture and possible rebuilds. This example has lasted into preservation looking very much as it would while working.

During the 1920s Leyland either saw a need for longer load carrying space, or were prevailed upon by lorry buyers to produce a longer lorry. The Leyland SQ2 was the result, with the driver in a semi-forward control position – thus providing more load space – and a capacity of 7 tons.

A Leyland SQ2 lorry saved and restored attending a vintage rally in the 1990s. The beginnings of full forward control can be seen in this frontal view. Leyland developed a longer SQ2 chassis with a second steering axle just ahead of the driving axle. What's new?

This picture shows a logging Leyland lorry in New Zealand, with a massive load. It may be an SQ2 type adapted by the operator for his own purposes, as it has the 1920s-style radiator and perforated front crossmember of the time. 'Rudimentary' would be a good description.

A picture of a C Type Leyland attending a Leyland Rally some years ago. It has been fitted with disc wheels and pneumatic tyres sometime in its life, which would bring some comfort for the driver, who still has a very basic cab.

An RAF Type which has gone through several updates, acquiring disc wheels and pneumatic tyres, along with electric lighting. The cab is still a bit basic, but not causing complaint from the driver on this fine July day.

By the 1930s Leyland production had moved to a range of lorries from the lightweight Cub up to the 3-axle Hippo, and subsequently, the 4-axle 8-wheeler, known as the Octopus. This old picture shows a cattle wagon on a Leyland Badger chassis. The radiator style is a throwback to the 1920s.

The Leyland Badger was offered as a bonneted type or in forward control, being originally a lightweight lorry, but the load capacity was uprated gradually to 6 tons. Electric lighting and a fully enclosed cab was a feature of these models.

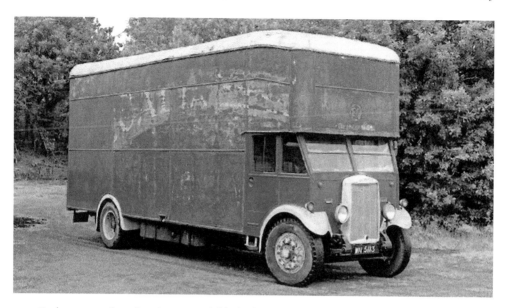

In the 1930s a low chassis was available for buses and coaches. This chassis was also available as a bulk-load carrier and designated with the name Llama. Large furniture vans, as seen here, were easily accommodated on the chassis. This one is in preservation after fairground use.

6,500, or more, Leyland Retrievers were designed and built by Leyland at the instigation of the War Office in the late 1920s and into the 1930s as 6x4 military vehicles for 3-ton loads. These lorries, and many more from other UK manufacturers, were the backbone of military transport at the outbreak of the Second World War. A similar, but lighter 6x4 type was known as the Terrier.

In time there would be a surplus of wartime vehicles as after the previous war, and the Retrievers would find their way into civilian service. This one has been heavily rebuilt for fairground service.

1930s Leyland production saw the emergence of heavyweight lorries built to the then-gross weights allowable for the time. The Leyland Beaver had a design gross weight of 12 tons, and was able to carry heavier loads than the Badger. It could also pull a trailer with a decent load capacity.

Here is a fine Leyland Beaver, which epitomises the lorry in preservation. The long and deep radiator is a prominent feature, giving a high front to the cab, which produces the trademark shallow windscreens.

Leylands often left the factory as chassis and scuttle, with coachbuilders building the cabs. While there was a similarity in shape, there was a wide variation in styles.

An almost similar Leyland Beaver tanker, which has been in preservation for a long time. The beat of the Leyland 4 cylinder engine is a sound all of its own. (Wobbe Reitsma)

Another Leyland Beaver of Ulster Transport working in the 1950s, evidenced by the Commer lorry in the background. The Beaver has a good load of steel bar supported by a single-axle bolster trailer.

The 3-axle, or 6-wheeler version of the 1930s Leyland range was known as the Hippo. The animal names were to be retained for several generations of Leyland lorries. The Hippo was available as 6x2 and 6x4 and was able to pull a trailer.

An early version of the Hippo, with the short radiator and the Leyland scroll badging, being loaded by hand. The scene brings to mind the old school exam type question of 'how long does it take three men to load a tipper lorry with 10 tons of gravel using No. 8 shovels?'

Leylands were bought by brewery companies who wanted to show to their customers they used quality lorries to deliver their quality beers. Marstons probably used this Hippo as a depot trunker rather than a delivery dray. It has been restored in immaculate order.

The 3-axle Leyland Hippo was the largest lorry in the Leyland range, but some users began to add an extra steering axle to increase the load capacity. Leyland, like other lorry makers, saw this as a viable addition to the range and the 4-axle Octopus took the top weight rating.

A fine example of a Leyland Octopus with the tall radiator and the low windscreens, seen in preservation. Many of these 8-wheelers were originally Hippos with a second steering axle added. 4-axle lorries had a legal gross running weight in the 1930s of 22 tons – 3 tons more than a 3-axle type.

In the 1930s the lightweight lorry market was catered for by Leyland with the Cub range. Cubs were available as bonneted, or forward control, and as 2-axle and 3-axle chassis; giving a fair choice to the user. This attractive preserved horsebox shows the bonneted style. (Glen McBirnie Collection)

This forward control Cub is an SKG2 model and was part of a fleet of Charles Alexander lorries carrying fish from Aberdeen. It had an unladen weight of just under 2.5 tons which allowed it to be driven up to 30 mph; hence its use on long-distance haulage.

Another Leyland Cub in preservation, seen here with a trailer, which might have been a little optimistic given the low power of the engine.

A short wheelbase Cub pictured in the service of a farm feed merchant in Ayrshire. The compact dimensions would have worked well in some of the farms visited. (Gillies Watson)

The Leyland Lynx was a larger development of the Cub and proved a popular lorry for 5- to 6-ton loads. This one, in the service of Bees of Hinckley, qualified for the 30 mph speed limit, but the box body would have been removable to keep the unladen weight under 2.5 tons.

A well set-up Lynx when new and about to go into service with Aberthaw Cement. The Lynx was the fore-runner of the post-Second World War Leyland Comet lorry.

An Edinburgh-registered Leyland Lynx, which had been used as a produce delivery lorry around Edinburgh; hence the running boards on the chassis.

A Leyland Lynx preserved in the colours of Joe Dean, a Halifax haulage contractor. It is a small, compact lorry well suited for urban collection and delivery work.

A similar Lynx in preservation, with a much more modern front bumper; the fitting of which is open to opinion.

The heavyweight Leylands were due to undergo a redesign, had not the Second World War broken out. The cab style would have been similar to this Beaver in the W. J. Riding fleet, and looked very modern for its time. Some wartime turntable fire appliances had this cab.

Leyland production, like most other vehicle manufacturers, was turned to munitions in the Second World War, with Comet tanks being a staple of the factory. However, lorry production did not stop and militarised Hippos were made. They were rated as 10-ton General Service lorries.

At the end of the Second World War Leyland returned to lorry and bus manufacture. The Leyland Beaver production line started with the IB type – or the Interim Beaver – which used the wartime-designed cab seen on military Hippos and pre-war components. One is pictured here on test.

Maintaining their tradition of using quality vehicles, many of the brewers took the Interim Beaver, and this one in preservation shows the rather rugged lines of the cab and the old fashioned radiator.

A lot of the military Hippos came into civilian service and, after modification, made good haulage lorries, if not a bit rudimentary. This picture depicts a heavily altered Hippo rebuilt as a tipper with an extra steering axle. It also has large section, modern single rear wheels.

A former military Hippo rebuilt as a tanker, and with civilian style wheels. It was probably exported.

The wartime Hippo was a useful lorry in the 1940s when new lorries were scarcely available. It would be relatively cheap and conversion to civilian use was fairly easy. Two examples of conversions are currently on preservation, this one recalling the erstwhile Davis Bros. business.

The military Hippo remained in forces service for a considerable time, probably due to their inherent ruggedness and simplicity, which explains the 1968/69 registrations applied to this pair in fairground service.

An Interim Beaver, which has also become part of the fairground circuit, allowing a large capacity body to be fitted and the ability to pull a substantial living van.

An ex-military Hippo which has been pressed into fairground service. It has been fitted with normal rear wheels and tyres, but retains military front tyres.

Leyland's new range of heavy lorries emerged in the late 1940s with a large – but rather Spartan – cab, which was fitted across the range. The Beaver seen in this photo had the newly developed o.600 engine and was rated as a drawbar model.

Very little embellishment was added to the new cab, except for the aluminium flashes. Some cabs had none at all. This preserved example was taking part in a Ted Hannon Northern Road Run some years ago.

Another fine preserved Beaver on the Tyne-Tees Road Run. This one has returned to work as a special hearse for road transport with funerals.

The post-war Beaver was always considered a useful, rugged lorry, which was capable of all kinds of work. They were frequently seen as cattle wagons, tippers, tankers, and fitted for many different uses, at home and abroad. This fine preserved Beaver looks just like a working lorry of the 1940s.

In the late 1940s there was a health drive by the then-UK government and a large number of Mass X-Ray vehicles were commissioned. Most of these were Leyland Beavers, and many became available in later years and were very suitable for restoration as lorries. This London 1951-registered lorry might have been one of them. (I. Lawson)

As in the 1930s range of heavy lorries there were 3-axle versions, still known as Hippos. They used the same engine as the Beaver and were rated for 19 tons laden, and later 20 tons. Haulage and tipper models were made. This one, in preservation, has a rather long tipper body on a fairly short wheelbase.

The heavyweight range was topped by the Octopus, as before. After the inception of British Road Services many of these 8-wheelers were sold to the nationalised haulage company. The Neild brothers have had this example in preservation for many years.

Well known in the south of England is this fine Leyland Octopus in the Taunton Cider livery. This model was known as the 22.O/1 type, meaning that it was rated for 22 tons gross weight. (Wobbe Reitsma)

The Hippo was a favourite lorry to convert to a wrecker. This one seems to have been out of use for a long time, but it turned up at a Cumbria Steam Gathering. Whether it went into preservation isn't known.

Sometimes the product carried on a lorry could be detrimental to it. Salt was one commodity that could cause problems, particularly with the lesser gauge metal in the cab. Boalloy was able to build part-fiberglass cabs on most chassis and this Leyland Octopus is so equipped.

This is a well-known Leyland Beaver, which has been in preservation for a long time. Latterly it was finished as a Caledonian contract lorry with Carnation Milk. It carries a later-style cab, which we will see later in the book.

By the early 1950s there was a requirement by the military for a new 6x6 artillery tractor to replace wartime AEC Matadors. The Leyland Martian was designed for this purpose and had a Rolls-Royce B81 8 cylinder engine. It apparently did not fulfil its task due its size and weight.

The Martian was also specified as a military heavy recovery and winch unit. It was fitted with a revolving crane and a winch capable of pulling 40 tons. As such, it was over 20 tons in weight. Some progressed into civilian hands, with the petrol hungry Rolls-Royce engines being replaced with large diesels.

Few examples of the Martian artillery tractor were used outside the military, but there are always exceptions. This one makes an impressive mobile home!

W. H. Malcolm is probably the largest Scottish road haulage firm in Scotland and has had various wreckers over the years. One such vehicle used the Leyland Martian as its basis, but the rebuild was drastic; a Scania cab was fitted, along with a Scania engine. What seemed like a good idea was too slow for motorway work – it was dismantled and the cab was used on a Scania III restoration.

In the late 1940s Leyland decided that a replacement lorry for the pre-war Lynx was needed to compete against the mass-produced 5- and 7-tonners. The design was a semi-forward control lorry with a propriety cab manufactured by Briggs Motor Bodies, also used on Ford and Dodge lorries. It could have a Leyland diesel or petrol engine. The diesel had a distinctive whistling sound.

The Leyland Comet was so-called after the wartime production of Comet tanks. It was available in short and long wheelbases, and as a tractor unit. It was rated as a 7-tonner for just under 11 tons gross weight.

An early restoration of a Leyland Comet was the Armstrong Cork Co. dropsider, which always looked good in the hands of the restorer – the late Bill Wilkinson of Gateshead. He is seen here driving his lorry at a vintage event in Dunbar about twenty-five years ago.

The Comet was popular as a middleweight artic unit when this type held sway among the heavier 6- and 8-wheelers. Most were fitted with the automatic trailer coupling, although this one has a fifth wheel.

As often before, there was a call to for the Comet to become forward control to allow more load space. Leyland designed such a chassis using the new style cab being fitted to the heavier Leylands at the time. It had the smaller O.350 engine, which later developed in stages to become the well-known O.400.

The forward control Comet was found to be an excellent lorry and eventually the bonneted type was phased out. This one from John Douglas – of Alston, in Cumbria – is a fine example in preservation.

In the 1950s Leyland tried to break into the Canadian truck market with a range of bonneted lorries, initially using a cab similar to the bonneted Comet. The bonnet was longer to accommodate larger engines. They were type-named as Buffalos and Bisons; this one being a Buffalo. Later models used a conventional (bonneted) International Harvester cab.

Midway through the 1950s Leyland upgraded the heavyweight types when a rise in gross vehicle weight was announced. The new range was topped by the Octopus, as usual, and a slightly restyled cab was used with a crossbarred radiator grill; known by some as the 'mouth organ' type. 24 tons was the new gross weight, and, after a wartime concession, 32 tons with a trailer.

Heavy articulation was only just catching on in the 1950s, but Leyland was able to supply a Beaver tractor unit for 24 tons gross weight. This is a fine example in preservation, taking part in an Ayrshire Road Run.

The Leyland Octopus was a well favoured chassis for fuel and oil haulage, and all the oil companies used them. It has to be said that most 8-wheelers found favour in this role because of their inherent stability. 8-wheelers of this era did not have braking on the second axle. (Wobbe Reitsma)

The Leyland heavyweight range also included the aptly named 3-axle Steer. This was a development from the 1930s to increase the load capacity without the weight of another drive axle. These lorries looked badly designed, as the drive axle had to be well to the rear to balance the load on the axles.

As the 1950s drew to an end, Leyland had a new design of lorries – albeit using the same type names. The earliest was a new version of the Comet with a propriety cab made by Motor Panels – soon to become known as the LAD, or Leyland-Albion-Dodge cab, which was also fitted on these other types.

The Comet was soon uprated, which brought about the Super Comet at 14 tons gross weight. Outwardly it was similar to the basic model, but had higher rated suspension and tyres. Compared to the previous Leyland cab, the LAD type was found to be rather cramped.

The Super Comet was found to be a good export model, which carried on the Leyland reputation in New Zealand where this one has been preserved. There isn't a lot of space in the cab for three people.

Another Leyland Comet in preservation. This one is part of the Donald Malcolm Heritage Fleet, and is kept in a purpose built museum at the Malcolm HQ, in Linwood. It has been finished in the W. H. Malcolm livery in use through the 1960s and 70s.

Here we see a superbly restored Comet taking part in a Tyne-Tees Road Run quite a number of years ago. Victor Harvey has a fleet of restored lorries and this one is one of the best. The driver is on the roof of the livestock box showing the collapsible third sheep deck.

The alternative to the Leyland Comet was the heavyweight Beaver, with a much larger engine and drawbar capability. Few were made for road haulage because of their weight, and road haulage was moving away from full trailers to articulation.

On the export side of Leyland's production, older style bonneted lorries were still being sold. This is a Super Beaver fitted with a ballast body arriving at the end of a Road Run, sometime in the 1990s. A few of this type were used by tipper operators in the UK when a short trailer allowed them to comply with overall length rules.

The Super Beaver was intended as an export model and had a tall radiator harking back to an earlier era, to allow better cooling and had basic easily-repaired cab components. This pair, having been fitted as tankers, are destined for Basrah, in Iraq.

Two Super Hippos showing the livery of ASG Transport Spedition from Sweden. They would normally run with trailers. ASG Transport Spedition is still a large Swedish business.

A Super Hippo found at the vintage lorry show at the Gaydon Motor Heritage Centre. It looks like a re-imported lorry as it would have been too large for UK roads at the time of its manufacture. Note the embellishments.

Australian lorry requirements were often in the large type, especially in the Outback areas. A Leyland lorry was developed for the Australian market, named Buffalo, which had a large Albion 900 cu. in. engine more commonly found in diesel railcars, and heavy haulage Scammells. Only a few were made.

From around 1960, the new Leyland heavy range began to appear with the LAD cab. The new range continued with the Beaver, Hippo, and Octopus designations, and this photo shows a beautifully restored Hippo in its native county of Lancashire. Hippos were more commonly seen as tippers.

A 1965 Beaver with a traditional haulage trailer. The cab fitted is the long door LAD type with a step ahead of the wheel to assist entry. This type of cab was also fitted to Albion lorries.

As before, the range topper was the Octopus, which, with a trailer, could run up to 32 tons gross. These new models were known as the Power Plus range and had an option of a larger O.680 Leyland diesel.

Fairground operators were enthusiastic users of 8-wheel lorries and this rather battered Leyland Octopus was probably a fuel tanker in an earlier use, where both types of operator appreciated the power and stability.

In the early 1960s Leyland took over the Standard-Triumph business, which produced cars and light vans. As a result of this merger the Leyland 2-tonner came into being. It made use of a rather ungainly version of the LAD cab and a Standard diesel engine. It was in direct competition with mass-produced light lorries and vans, and was not successful.

The Leyland 2-tonner was uprated to a 2.5-tonner and was then known as the Leyland 90. The uprate in capacity did not promote a better sales figure against the mass produced cheaper lightweights, and the model was quietly removed from the range.

Another use of the LAD cab style was on the Super Comet and Bear 6-wheelers, intended for tipper and concrete mixer work. These were very similar lorries and could be mistaken for the venerable Albion Reiver, popular as a tipper.

In 1964 the government raised permissible weights for lorries and increased the legal dimensions. To meet the new rules Leyland embarked on a new range of lorries known as the Freightline models. The Super Comet was included and was updated with the new Ergomatic cab, to be seen on heavier Leylands, AECs, and some Albions.

The Octopus models lost out in the new gross weight due to impossible wheelbase dimensions. This one was plated at 26 tons gross and had a turning circle that could catch out the unwary because of the long wheelbase to achieve the gross weight.

The Ergomatic-cabbed Leyland artics had now taken the top weight spot in the range, and could operate at 32 tons gross with a tri-axle trailer. This Alex Anderson Leyland is a Badger, which was introduced as a lighter-weight version of the Beaver tractor unit.

The Ergomatic, or Freightline range also had long wheelbase Beavers for drawbar use. As in previous Leyland heavy lorry ranges, there was a similarity of parts across the models.

In the course of time Leyland produced a Beaver with a semi-automatic gearbox, based on the gearbox that had been fitted to buses for many years. Outwardly it looked no different, but had a short pedestal lever for gear changing. They were known colloquially as 2 Pedal Beavers.

Another Alex Anderson Leyland, this time a Beaver, which has remained in British Copper Refiners colours. It is seen taking part in an Ayrshire Road Run near Portpatrick, in Galloway.
(G. Carpenter)

A lot of the long wheelbase Beavers were used for special purposes, and this one was built as an aircraft refueller, at a higher gross weight than road vehicle. This one operated at Prestwick Airport, near the sea, and suffered badly from the corrosive salty air.

The Leyland Beaver could operate at 32 tons, but only practically with a tri-axle trailer. The Reid's Transport Beaver is seen in this combination with a York Castella-Beam platform. A twin steer version of the Beaver was conceived, to run with tandem trailers. Only a few were made.

The Ergomatic Beaver was a compact tractor unit in short wheelbase for and many became tow wagons. This one is pictured in service with the Southern National Bus Company. It is a 2 Pedal type and is presently in preservation in Ayrshire.

A further preserved Beaver in Ayrshire is this one which was part of the William Johnstone collection, running in his late father's colours.

After a working life in haulage the Ergomatic Beaver wasn't the first choice of fairground operators, probably because of the amount of corrosion that would appear on these cabs. This one was looking good at the time of the photo, at Ayr Races Gold Cup weekend.

By the 1970s Leyland had developed a new engine range with a fixed cylinder head to eradicate cylinder head gasket failure. It was fitted to the new Lynx, Bison, and Buffalo; known as the 500 Series, after the engine capacity. This is a Lynx with an updated cab, also used on the other models, and the last of the Leyland Super Comets.

As the 1970 era began Leyland Motors merged with British Motor Holdings (BMH), which was in essence the producer of BMC cars and lorries. The merger was to support BMH, which was struggling financially. To this end BMC lorries were badged as Leylands in 1972, as this Irish Leyland FG lightweight shows.

The BMC range of small lorries was what the Leyland 90 was competing with, among others. It was odd to see the name Leyland on what had always been either an Austin or a Morris.

The heavy end of the BMC range included Mastiffs, Boxers, and Lairds. This is a V8 engined Mastiff, which made a middleweight artic at 28 tons gross. The Leyland name has been applied here, by the factory, in a rather amateurish fashion in place of BMC.

The Mastiff was a popular chassis for conversion to a tipper in Malta because of the large V8 engine. Mastiffs also had a more substantial chassis based on that of the Guy Big J – another make drawn into the Leyland conglomerate with BMC.

The Mastiff, along with the Boxer, had become part of the Redline range – a name applied to the former BMC models. Here is a long wheelbase model pausing on a journey in the West Country. (P. Crang)

A lighter Boxer which has seen use as a furniture van. This type replaced the former BMC Laird, itself based on the original BMC FJ type. They usually had a BMC Diesel engine. This cab was the first mass produced tilt cab offered in the UK.

In replacement of the older BMC FG models a lightweight range known as the Terrier came into production. The Terrier used 4 and 6 cylinder diesels of BMC origin.

The old BMC cab was update in 1972 with a new front panel and the Leyland name boldly placed below the windscreen. This is a Boxer for 16 tons gross, and was fitted with a Perkins engine.

A similar Boxer to illustrate the range of wheelbases available on the type. Having reached preservation the owner has adorned it with various motifs and badges professing his allegiance.

The Boxer range was exported to Australia and many other countries. This Australian version, with 'roo bars, has a good load of recycling material. (Bob Tuck)

The Terrier also had the new cab style. Improvements were made to the interior at the same time, but essentially it remained just like the original. Cab tilting was easy after long bolts were removed, but they had to be kept tight to prevent them falling out.

The Terrier was usually a 7.5-ton lorry and did not come into the LGV licencing sphere, so they were popular with farmers and small business, where most people could drive them.

This Terrier was part of a small fleet of lorries frequently engaged on airfreight and its higher speed limit would have allowed faster journey times for urgent goods.

After the European lorry-makers obtained a foothold in the UK lorry market, Leyland came up with a lorry range in competition, named the Marathon. Essentially, it was a higher powered chassis, with a former AEC engine – the AV760. Cummins and Rolls-Royce engines were options.

The Marathon could be specified as tractor units with 4x2 and 6x4 drive. A long wheelbase drawbar unit was also available. Unfortunately, the cab was virtually a raised version of the original Ergomatic cab and although it had a flat floor, it was cramped and basic. A sleeper version became a later option.

This is the drawbar version, restored and rallied by Chris Hirons, from the Midlands, with a rest style sleeper cab.

William (Billy) Bowie converted a former Marathon military fuel tanker by cutting down the wheelbase and fitting skip loader equipment. It is used as a promotional vehicle at various events.

While having the appearance of an 8-wheeler Marathon tipper, is it a 6-wheel Marathon converted by adding a second steering axle, or an existing 8-wheeler with a cab conversion? An interesting vehicle used on Cyprus, nonetheless. (A. Syme)

A more conventional Marathon with a tri-axle tanker trailer waiting for a load of the world famous Johnnie Walker Whisky.

The Marathon 2 was an improved version of the original, but still retained the old Ergomatic-style cab. This is Steve Greenwood, from Manchester, coming into a lunch stop on an Ayrshire Road Run.

Albion had been a Leyland subsidiary since 1951 and marketed its products as Albions until 1972 when, along with the BMC types, they were rebranded as Leylands. This is a Leyland Clydesdale with the BMC style cab, then being made at the former BMC factory at Bathgate. The former Albions were designated at the Blue Line range.

The Albion Reiver had been a popular lorry from early production and was still a good seller when it became a Leyland Blue Line member. The popularity of this lorry was in its light weight.

The Albion Reiver had always been a popular 6-wheel livestock carrier and as a Leyland it continued the tradition. James Kinnear's Reiver is seen loading in the former Stirling Kildean Market.

Another former Albion was the Chieftain middleweight. Under Leyland badging it became a middleweight lorry at 13.5 tonnes gross, or a lightweight artic; used in large numbers by Royal Mail. Truck Plant Services, of Paisley, have this one in preservation.

W. H. Malcolm used older lorries as yard shunters, and this Leyland Clydesdale – with 10 stud wheels – may have been converted to an artic unit, in house.

The Leyland Clydesdale was most often seen as a long platform lorry, and Whitecairn Transport had a number of them on livestock haulage. Their strong, straight chassis made them ideal load carriers, but perhaps slightly underpowered by the Leyland O.400 engine derivative.

The last of the Ergomatic cabs were found on the Lynx, Buffalo, Bison, and Octopus range of the late 1970s. The cab had been raised a few inches to cope with taller engines and had a restyled front, with the headlights placed in the bumper. This is Joe Bradley's excellent restoration in Portpatrick Harbour.

Joe Bradley also restored a Bison tipper, which had been new to the family quarrying business. It is seen turning at a junction on an Ayrshire Road Run.

The Bison was a good basis for an aircraft refueller, with its low-set cab, allowing it to drive under aircraft wings. With suitable gearing it would be designed to run at a higher gross weight in airports, while pulling a sizeable trailer. (Bob Tuck)

The Leyland Octopus had been taken off the market in the late 1960s, as legislation had ruled against 8-wheelers in general. A later change of rules made the 8-wheeler a viable proposition at 30 tonnes gross, and Leyland re-introduced the model, which was essentially similar to the Bison, with a fourth axle.

The Lynx was seen as a direct replacement for the former Leyland Super Comet, but it did not do so well in competition with the contemporary Clydesdale.

Another Lynx livestock lorry turned out in the traditional Scottish livery of James Cairns & Son.

This may or may not be a Leyland Bison! It has the 500 range front panels and bumper, but the cab is set at the standard height. Showmen are well known for their modifications and the lorry just might be an AEC Marshal!

Towards the end of the 1970s Leyland were formulating a brand-new range of lorries to be known as the T45s. A lot of rationalisation was taking place, including the ceasing of production of AEC, Guy, former Albion and BMC types. All production was to be centred on the T45 range, which encompassed everything from 7.5-tonners to heavyweight abnormal load movers. This is a Roadtrain running at 32 tonnes gross from the Harry Lawson fleet.

The T45 Roadtrain proved a good competitor to the imports from Europe and were to be seen in all types of work. This WCF (West Cumberland Farmers) curtainsider is seen at their Ayr depot.

T. & M. Catto, a refrigerated haulier from Aberdeen, was an early user of the Roadtrain; running from Aberdeen to the London markets. (K. Durston)

Like previous Leyland product lines the T45 range had an 8-wheeler model known as the Constructor 8. It took a lot of its design from the former Scammell Routeman, and became known as a rugged chassis for tipper work. Mellings of Preston had previously ran the older Scammells.

As always, the 8-wheeler lorry was renowned for stability and this former Scottish Borders livestock haulier used a Constructor 8 as a double-deck cattle transporter. It was one of the largest rigid livestock lorries on the road.

The T45 cab was wide and spacious, and available with a sleeper cab, but the Forestry Commission, in their wisdom, had this somewhat ungainly 'upstairs bedroom' grafted to the roof. Load space would be the governing factor as a rear sleeper cab would have encroached on that area.

The Constructor 8 was produced with the wide T45 cab, as found on the Roadtrain. A High Datum cab could also be fitted to certain models, which raised the can about 10 to 12 inches.

Some operators thought the wide T45 cab made the 8-wheeler chassis a little overweight and sought a lighter day cab. The solution was to fit the narrower cab from the lighter T45 family, as seen on this Scottish Oils Constructor 8.

The 6-wheel T45 member was well-received by most former Leyland users and it was popular in most lines of haulage. Geordie Bell had this one on livestock haulage, and many were used by tipper operators.

The Constructor 6 was a popular chassis for mounting concrete mixers. Barmix ran a small fleet of them, some being convertible to demountable tippers.

The Freighter was the medium-to-heavy 4-wheeler in the T45 range and was used in many forms. This short wheelbase tipper was a rarity in its time, as most tippers had become 3- and 4-axle types by then.

Like the Leyland Clydesdales and the Comets, the Freighter was well thought of as a livestock carrier, although by this time, like many other haulage operations, larger lorries were the norm. This is a Freighter 16.13.

Milk collection was also seeing the need for larger tankers and 6-wheelers were coming into use. These had a tendency to damage farmyard surfaces with tyre scrub, and twin steer conversions were tried. The idea was good, prompting a move to 8-wheelers with steerable rear axles.

Lightweight Freighters were offered by Leyland and here is a 13 tonne version, which has seen a fair bit of use. It was a BRS Contracts lorry, working in Glasgow.

Something that has become a rare sight is the coal roundsman's lorry. British Fuels had a fleet of lightweight Freighters working across the country. The T45 family resemblance is clear right down the range.

The heavy T45 models were taken quite enthusiastically in Europe and this drawbar outfit was used by Transports Legrand in France. It has the high datum cab but retains the same interior height. (C. Baron)

The Roadtrain was not often seen in the UK as a drawbar model. Mothercare had some 17.25 drawbar outfits, which were built with demountable bodies for increased versatility. This one was rated as a 250 bhp model, which was not a lot of power for such a combination.

At the lower end of the T45 range was the Roadrunner, specifically for the 7.5-tonner market. The model was introduced in a blaze of publicity, being driven on two wheels. It was readily taken up by the market it was aimed at.

The Roadrunner was a direct replacement for the Terrier 7.5-tonner, and was used, like the Terrier, by farmers and small businesses. The window – sometimes termed the dog's window – was an attempt to help the drivers while parking; a throwback to the old BMC FG style cab.

British Telecom and the Post Office were large users of Roadrunners, which were to be seen right across the country. At that time an LGV driving licence was not needed for this class of lorry, making the Roadrunner a class leader.

Not being a large lorry, the Roadrunner has not made a big impact on the fairground circuit. This one, with a fairly substantial Luton body, and pulling a trailer, is probably just in scope for the gross train weight of 8.25 tonnes.

While Leyland was producing the T45 range, a large bonneted Landtrain model was being produced as an export lorry. Most were 6x4 drive and a large fleet was sent to the Falkland Islands to rebuild the damaged airport. This brand-new one was taking part in a Truckshow. The former BMC cab was used on these lorries, much adapted to suit.

Some of the Falkland Islands' Landtrains were returned to the UK and went to open-cast mining operations, where intensive off-road bulk haulage was required. This 30.29 Landtrain seems to be being driven with some vigour. (Bob Tuck)

This Landtrain was used within the British Leyland research and development facility at Leyland, and was described as a power measurement apparatus; being dragged around the test track by research teams.

Some of the 6x4 units found their way to Malta where they were put to use. This one may have been in the Falklands, fitted as a mixer. (P. Crang)

In the 1980s Leyland saw a need for simpler export lorries, without modern electronics and sophisticated systems required by law in the UK, along the lines of former Albion and Leyland export models. This idea manifested itself in the export-only Comet and Super Comet, built as no-frills lorries.

The range included long and short wheelbase types, easily repaired away from service centres. The Super Comet was a 3-axle version. A Scottish tipper operator opined that if he was allowed to buy and run them, he would have an entire fleet of Super Comets! A bonneted type known as the Landmaster was also developed.

Also on the Leyland agenda in the 1980s was a new type of military vehicle and cargo handling system. This was to become the Demountable Rack Off-load and Pick-up System (DROPS) 8x6 army truck. It was developed by Scammell, but by the time it entered service it carried Leyland DAF badging. (P. Crang)

Around the same time a new 4x4 general service military truck specification was put out to tender. Leyland was awarded the contract to build this truck, which was a 4- to 5-tonner to replace the many Bedford 4x4 trucks in military service. It had a cab using parts from the Roadrunner and other T45 components, and a Cummins engine. It entered service badged as a Leyland DAF.

In recent years the military have been upgrading their vehicles at shorter life intervals, and the 4x4 type has found its way into various civilian uses, as seen here with this pair forming part of Pinder's Circus transport. In the military they are being replaced by M.A.N. trucks. (P. Crang)

After the merger with British Motor Holdings, and becoming the property of the British government, Leyland's fortunes took a downhill pattern. A decision was reached by the government in 1987 to sell the truck-building side to DAF Trucks. From that year all Leylands were badged as Leyland DAF.

The T45 range was continued with the old names being superseded by type numbers, in which the Roadtrain and the Constructor 8 became the Leyland DAF 80. This one is in a second life on Malta. (P. Crang)

The former Freighter became the Leyland DAF 60, as seen on this twin steer milk tanker in Aberdeen.

Another Leyland DAF 60, with a modified T45 cab to allow easy access for its crew. Along with the new badging, the front panels were restyled to fit in with the then DAF corporate style.

Many Leyland DAF 80 heavyweights were to be found on Malta, and this one, built as a wrecker, is coincidentally pulling another Leyland; one of the last bus models that used the revived Lynx name.

The lightweights were given the same treatment and this Leyland DAF 50 would have been a Freighter at the lower end of that type's weight scale.

The familiar Roadrunner became the Leyland DAF 45, again with the corporate face-lift.

Over the years Leylands have been used for a great variety of uses, but in some instances not the purpose they were designed for. After the Second World War, new lorries were difficult to acquire and compromises had to happen. This is a former 1930s Leyland London bus converted to a beaver-tail lorry.

The Vanwall Formula One racing team was famous in the 1950s and had a purpose-built transporter, built on a Leyland Royal Tiger Worldmaster bus chassis; an underfloor engined type, to utilise as much load space as possible.

A similar method of thinking applied to these New Zealand-operated car transporters, built on Leyland bus chassis. The driving position was lowered to allow a low mobile crane type cab, which facilitate two cars being carried above it.

Leyland built an experimental vehicle on such a chassis, as did some other lorry makers, but the idea did not catch on. The Leyland was used as a foundation chassis for brake research, and is now in preservation.

Not so much a special use lorry, but inserted to show how large a van body could be built on a Leyland Comet. It started life with the well-known and oldest UK haulage company – The Shore Porters Society of Aberdeen (Established 1498) – then became part of the fairground circuit.

About as far as you can get from the original design of the former BMC FG lorry. An integral van body and cab of somewhat rudimentary design, which may have been an amateur build of a mobile home. Either way, it looks neatly built.

When is a bus not a bus? When it becomes a tow wagon. Many older buses were converted for towing duties, and this Leyland Leopard was treated thus by the Scottish Bus Group.

An interesting project that did not bear fruit. It would be part of a Leyland bid for a military contract, possibly abroad. It has heavy axles and 6x6 drive for an expected heavy duty use.

The Ergomatic cab was never very spacious, but this one takes the biscuit. Obviously damaged on the nearside or rotten with corrosion, we see an unlikely half-cab conversion.

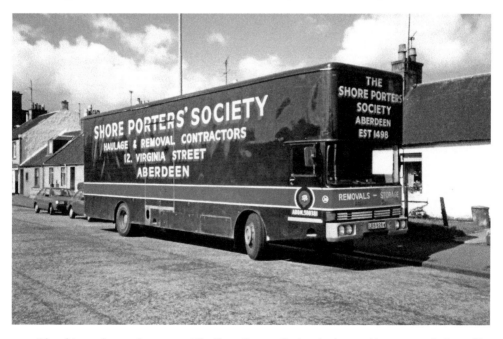

The ultimate box or Luton van. The Shore Porters Society had several large pantechnicons like this, built on underfloor-engined bus chassis. This one is based on a Leyland Leopard chassis. It must have been nice to drive with the engine noise subdued by the bodywork and load.

Various engineering companies modified normal production lorries for special purposes. This Freighter has been converted for snowplough/gritter use in winter and would be available as a tipper at other times.

The badging on this Constructor suggests it is a former 8-wheeler built for 30 tons gross, but only has three axles. Why this should be is not known, as a proper Constructor 6 chassis could have been specified for the job.

Whether this is considered a Leyland or a Scammell is open to opinion. It is certainly a Scammell-developed military lorry, converted as a snowplough/gritter.

Some operators were not keen on the rear suspension layout of the Constructors, when they were not made available with a 4-spring non-reactive bogie. This operator took the front of two lighter T45 Cruiser artic units, extended the chassis, fitted the rear suspension he favoured, and came up with a pair of tippers to his own specification.

As the Roadtrain was never built by Leyland or Scammell as a 4x4, this one, for use at Birmingham Airport, would have been engineered by a specialist company. It was intended for runway snow-clearing.

A project by Leyland in the late 1960s was the building of a small number of gas turbine-engined lorries, with a view to this type of power being used in the future. It was not a great success. One of the research units has survived, being restored by Tony Knowles.

Last but not least is a Leyland Sisu. This was the result of Leyland supplying Boxer chassis to Sisu as a downward extension of their own range. No sales were forthcoming and the Leylands were returned to the UK. Some may have ended up in Turkey as 'Tonka Trucks'.